LIGHTNING BOLT BOOKS™

Explore Venus

Liz Milroy

Lerner Publications ◆ Minneapolis

PAGE PLUS +

Scan the QR code on page 21 to see Venus in 3D!

Lerner Publications Company
An imprint of Lerner Publishing Group, Inc.
241 First Avenue North
Minneapolis, MN 55401 USA

For reading levels and more information, look up this title at www.lernerbooks.com.

Main body text set in Billy Infant regular.
Typeface provided by SparkType.

Editor: Brianna Kaiser **Lerner team:** Sue Marquis

Library of Congress Cataloging-in-Publication Data

Names: Milroy, Liz, author.
Title: Explore Venus / Liz Milroy.
Other titles: Lightning bolt books. Planet explorer.
Description: Minneapolis, MN : Lerner Publications, 2021 | Series: Lightning bolt books - Planet explorer | Includes bibliographical references and index. | Audience: Ages 6-9 | Audience: Grades 2-3 | Summary: "See how Venus compares to all the neighboring planets. Cool facts and scientific information will help young readers explore the hottest planet in our solar system"— Provided by publisher.
Identifiers: LCCN 2020019906 (print) | LCCN 2020019907 (ebook) | ISBN 9781728404158 (library binding) | ISBN 9781728423678 (paperback) | ISBN 9781728418513 (ebook)
Subjects: LCSH: Venus (Planet)—Juvenile literature.
Classification: LCC QB621 .M554 2021 (print) | LCC QB621 (ebook) | DDC 523.42—dc23

LC record available at https://lccn.loc.gov/2020019906
LC ebook record available at https://lccn.loc.gov/2020019907

Manufactured in the United States of America
1-48473-48987-9/10/2020

Table of Contents

All about Venus

This planet is entirely covered with clouds. You're on Venus! It's the brightest planet in our solar system.

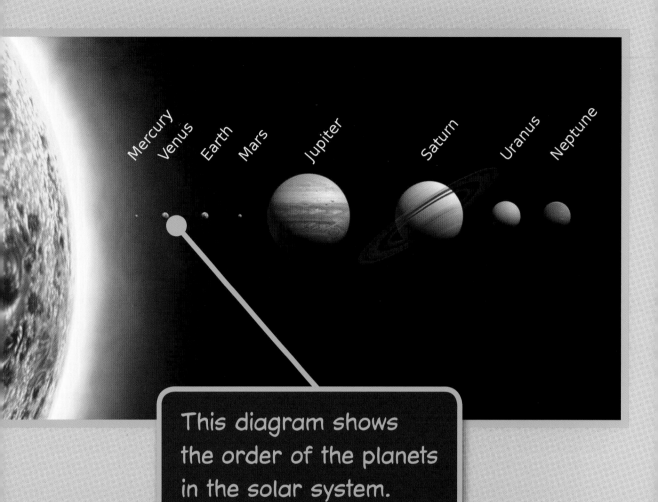

Mercury Venus Earth Mars Jupiter Saturn Uranus Neptune

This diagram shows the order of the planets in the solar system.

Venus is the second planet in the solar system. It's about 67 million miles (108 million km) away from the sun.

Left to right: Earth, Mars, Venus, and Mercury are the rocky planets in the solar system.

Like Mercury, Earth, and Mars, Venus is called a rocky planet. Rocky planets are smaller than other kinds of planets and are mostly solid.

Venus and Earth are almost the same size. Venus is about 7,521 miles (12,104 km) across, and Earth is 7,918 miles (12,743 km) across.

Earth and Venus are sometimes called planetary twins because they are almost the same size.

The sun is about 864,400 miles (1.39 million km) wide. Over one million Venuses could fit inside the sun.

Venus is much smaller than the sun.

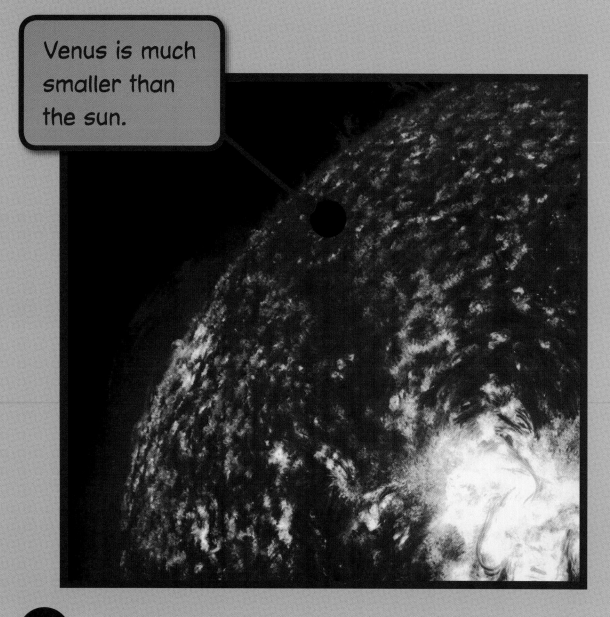

Venus has a really thick atmosphere.

Venus is the hottest planet in our solar system. This is because its really thick atmosphere traps heat. Its temperature can be higher than 880°F (471°C).

What's in a Name?

People in ancient times noticed Venus shined bright in the night sky. They named it after the Roman goddess Venus. She was the goddess of love and beauty.

Roman goddess Venus

Venus can be seen from Earth without a telescope.

Venus can only be seen from Earth around sunrise and sunset. Since Venus shows up in the morning and evening, people sometimes call it the morning star and the evening star.

Living on Venus

Venus would be a difficult place to visit. Its atmosphere is made mostly of carbon dioxide, and it rains sulfuric acid. You would not be able to breathe.

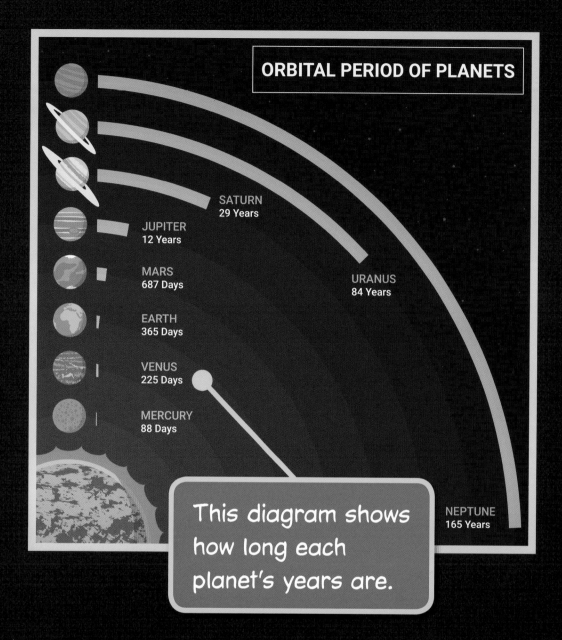

ORBITAL PERIOD OF PLANETS

SATURN
29 Years

JUPITER
12 Years

MARS
687 Days

URANUS
84 Years

EARTH
365 Days

VENUS
225 Days

MERCURY
88 Days

NEPTUNE
165 Years

This diagram shows how long each planet's years are.

On Venus, a day is longer than a year. A day is almost 243 Earth days long, but a year only takes 225 Earth days.

From the surface of Venus, the sun would rise in the west.

Venus spins in the opposite direction of Earth and most other planets. On Venus, the sun appears to rise in the west and set in the east.

Earth has seasons because it is tilted on an axis. Venus's tilt is so large that the planet is nearly upside down. Its extreme tilt causes Venus to have no seasons and to spin backward.

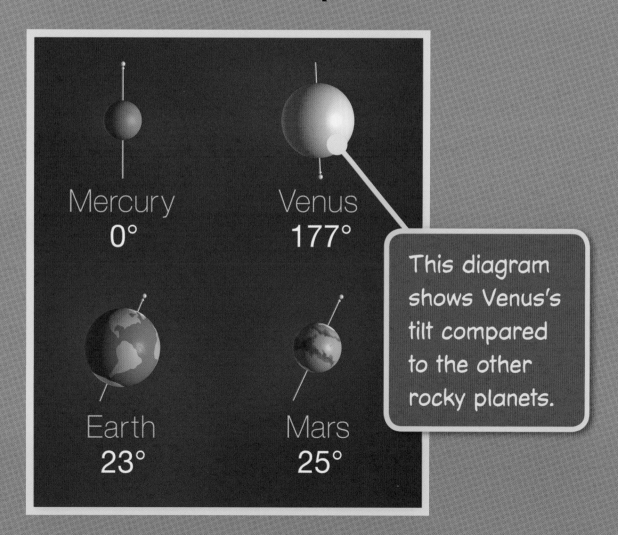

Mercury
0°

Venus
177°

Earth
23°

Mars
25°

This diagram shows Venus's tilt compared to the other rocky planets.

Checking Out Venus

Venus's harsh environment has destroyed every spacecraft that has landed on its surface. But astronomers continue to send spacecraft to explore Venus.

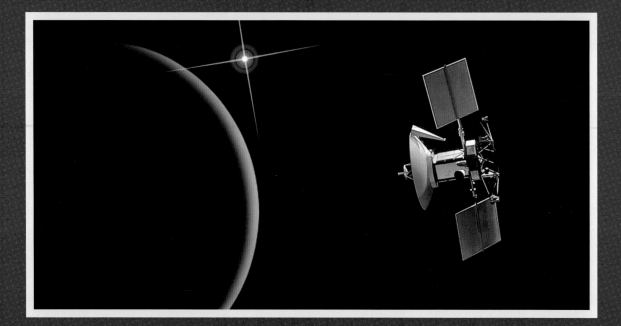

Venera 1 was the first spacecraft to fly by Venus.

In 1961, *Venera 1* became the first spacecraft to fly by Venus. The *Magellan* spacecraft orbited Venus from 1990 to 1994. It was the first spacecraft to image the entire surface of Venus.

Akatsuki, a Japanese spacecraft, left Earth in 2010. It reached Venus in 2015.

Akatsuki began its journey toward Venus in 2010.

This is a model of *Akatsuki*.

Astronomers study missions like *Akatsuki* to learn more about the weather on Venus. Will you find out more one day?

Planet Facts

Uranus and Venus are the only planets in our solar system that spin backward.

Since Venus is near Earth and almost the same size, early astronomers thought it might be home to alien life. These made-up people from Venus were called Venusians, or Venerians.

Most of the craters on Venus are at least a mile (1.6 km) wide. That's because only big meteors land on Venus. Smaller ones burn up before they can land and create craters.

Like Mercury, Venus doesn't have any moons.

Space Story

Venus is covered in craters, mountains, and volcanoes. Most of the volcanoes on Venus stopped erupting around three hundred million years ago. That was so long ago that dinosaurs weren't even walking on Earth yet. Most of Venus's craters, mountains, and volcanoes are named after famous women of Earth.

Scan the QR code to the right to see Venus in 3D!

Glossary

astronomer: a scientist who looks at stars, planets, and other things in outer space

atmosphere: a layer of gas that surrounds a planet

axis: an invisible line that Venus turns around

orbit: the path taken by one body circling around another body

rocky planet: a planet made up of mostly rocks or metals. Mercury, Venus, Earth, and Mars are all rocky planets.

solar system: our sun and everything that orbits around it

spacecraft: a ship made by people to move through space

year: the amount of time it takes for a planet to orbit its star once

Learn More

Goldstein, Margaret J. *Discover Venus*. Minneapolis: Lerner Publications, 2019.

Milroy, Liz. *Explore Jupiter*. Minneapolis: Lerner Publications, 2021.

NASA for Students
https://www.nasa.gov/stem/forstudents/k-4/index.html

NASA Space Place: All about Venus
https://spaceplace.nasa.gov/all-about-venus/en/

Nichols, Michelle. *Astronomy Lab for Kids: 52 Family-Friendly Activities*. Beverly, MA: Quarry, 2016.

Index

Photo Acknowledgments

Image credits: NASA, pp. 4, 19; WP/Wikimedia Commons (CC BY-SA 3.0), p. 5; Lsmpascal/Wikimedia Commons (CC BY-SA 3.0), p. 6; NASA/Ames/JPL-Caltech, p. 7; NASA/SDO, AIA (CC BY 2.0), p. 8; Meli thev/Wikimedia Commons (CC BY-SA 4.0), p. 9; The J. Paul Getty Museum, Los Angeles, p. 10; ESO/Y. Beletsky (CC BY 4.0), p. 11; NASA/JPL, pp. 12, 14, 16; Andramin/Shutterstock.com, p. 13; NASA/JPL-Caltech/Richard Barkus, p. 15; Armael/Wikimedia Commons (CCO 1.0), p. 17; Naritama/Wikimedia Commons (CC BY-SA 3.0), p. 18.

Cover: NASA/JPL.